Forever Victorious

Get Unstuck, Embrace your Purpose, and Win in Life

LILLIAN MUTAVA

© 2019 Divine Works Publishing
Forever Victorious

ALL RIGHTS RESERVED. No part of this publication may be reproduced, stored in a retrieval system, or transmitted in any form or by any means, electronic, mechanical, photocopying, recording or otherwise without the prior permission of the publisher or in accordance with the provisions of the Copyright, Designs, and Patents Act 1988 or under the terms of any license permitting limited copying issued by the Copyright Licensing Agency.

The views expressed in this work are solely those of the author and do not necessarily reflect the views of the publisher, the publisher hereby disclaims any responsibility for them.

ISBN-13: 978-1-949105-13-1 (paperback)
ISBN-13: 978-1-949105-14-8 (eBook)

Published by:
Divine Works Publishing, LLC
Royal Palm Beach, Florida USA

www.DivineWorksPublishing.com
561-990-BOOK (2665)

Contents

Introduction: Relentless Tenacity! *VII*

Part I
VULNERABLE MOLTING

Ch 1 Change Your Mind–Shed Plumage *3*
Ch 2 Forgiveness, an Act of Love–Rejuvenated Talons *9*
Ch 3 Get Unstuck–Rise Above Challenges and Seasonal Changes *17*

Part II
EMERGE SHARPER AND STRONGER

Ch 4 God Chose You–Powerful Vision And Revelation *25*
Ch 5 Identity in Christ–Your Transformation is Solidified *29*
Ch 6 Uncover Your Potential–Significance & Relevance of Your Wings *33*

Part III
THE WIND AND YOUR WINGS

Ch 7 Pursue Purpose–Spread Your Wings You Have a Bigger Purpose *41*
Ch 8 Settle in His Presence–Conserve Your Energy, Use The Wind *47*
Ch 9 God's Wisdom–Wait on the Wind Thermals *53*

Part IV
SOAR AGAIN

Ch 10 Celebrate You–You are Designed to be Limitless *61*
Ch 11 Grace Wins–The Beauty of Form Under the Influence of Freedom *65*
Ch 12 Break Free–Flight of Rebirth *69*
Ch 13 Birth New Dreams–Rise To Greater Heights *75*

Dream Again! *81*

About the Author *91*

INTRODUCTION

Relentless Tenacity

We do not see things as they are; we see things as we are.
-Anais Nim

The fact that you're reading this book reveals that you are seeking to overcome life's detours and get on the course towards living out your life's purpose. At this moment, you may be wrestling with the question: "What am I supposed to do with my life?" For some of us, we have done what we were supposed to do, or what seemed like the best options for a successful life.

However, unfortunately for many, it doesn't turn out to be a path to a fulfilling and rewarding life. Life may seem different from what you planned. Events catch you off guard for a moment while others weaken or eventually break you. You quietly question God's plan and purpose in your life. It's never too late to get unstuck, pursue your purpose, and transform your life.

Too many of us have been rejected, betrayed, heart-broken and left to deal with broken dreams. While this is an uncomfortable place to find oneself, when we are grounded in the knowledge of God's word, we can endure life's detours and remain victorious despite these traumatic experiences.

Like you, I've experienced the pain and confusion that is

associated with betrayal, rejection, and broken dreams that can lead to self-doubt. Experiences that push you to question God's plan for your life. For example, is what I am doing today part of God's plan? Am I living a fulfilling and rewarding life?

You see, for years my life was complacent and mediocre. It felt unfulfilling and yielded little to no reward. Every day I believed I was living to the fullest of my potential. However, deep inside of me, was a yearning that I was made for more. Although, I had followed the blueprint for what I was supposed to do, based on my upbringing and what my environment dictated—pursued a career, got educated, worked hard to find my space in the corporate world—I always had this unsettling thought, was this all that God had planned for me?

My upbringing is rooted in a deep rich African culture that is grounded in the word of God. A daughter of a Pentecostal Pastor and a caring hell-breaking prayer warrior mother. So, there was little to no thought in my head that I was created to win, thrive, and live to the fullest of my potential but the questions always lingered. How was I supposed to live victoriously? And not just victorious because I was getting paid well at the corporate level or I was well educated at my age, but many times, I would envision my life to be larger than where I was at that moment in life.

As a teenager, I embarked on a new journey. I left the comfort of my upbringing to pursue a higher education. The idea was to leave my familiar surroundings and embrace something new. I was driven by the pursuit to seize a better opportunity in life that would pivot me to the next level of success in life.

Even though I had the opportunity to expand my wings to soar. My upbringing, which was sheltered under the simplicity of joyful, vibrant, friendly and hospitable African culture, didn't prepare me fully to the new reality I was facing. It was so imperative that I changed the lens which I viewed life from.

Out of curiosity, I embraced my newfound freedom. You see, as a university student far away from home, I was free to make my own decisions. However, the desire to succeed continued to propel me to remain focused on attaining a college degree.

One thing for sure was, I wasn't prepared for the harsh realities my new environment presented. I had to survive my new normal. The individual mindset "survival of the fittest". The reality I assimilated in Africa "it takes a village to raise a child" was no longer my reality. Even though I had support from my family from afar , I had to adjust and make changes earlier on.

As I pursued a successful life, I failed to realize that my unrenewed and clouded mindset was affecting every decision of my life. There was a price tag associated with every choice I made. With every decision, there is a resulting consequence, and that, my friend, is where life gets complicated.

My decisions consistently opened the door to mediocrity and complacent relationships with individuals who were struggling with multiple issues in life. These relationships over time would end up in betrayal, brokenness and defeat. As human beings, we want it all. We want to feel loved, cared for, and move on from one experience to every other experience that life can offer us, but we don't want to pay the bill for this morning's choices and yesterday's behaviors.

Living with a complacent and mediocre mindset is self-defeating, naïve, and ignorant. The fact that I was educated and was raised in a good home still required me to understand my purpose in life. The lack of knowledge in what my purpose was in life continued to influence my decisions. You are what you think. Your thoughts become your actions and your actions become your character.

You see, with this type of mindset coupled with the naivety of trusting people too fast, lacking the knowledge in my identity, produced the same cycles in my life. Not too long after, I began to connect the dots in my experiences and it unlocked something new.

We've all had experiences in life that triggered a deep desire to discover our life purpose. These triggers vary for each of us based on the personal crisis–job loss, divorce, relocation, business failure, a relationship ending and many more. My trigger moment was defined at a routine nail appointment that lasted less than five minutes.

A defining moment occurred when I was approached by a lady at the salon as she prepared to depart. She spoke to me and pierced through the inner turmoil I was experiencing. She instinctively gravitated towards me and spoke with such conviction. She had a message to deliver. Her message was clear and only God would have sent her.

She uttered these words to me, "I will only say what the Lord wants me to tell you. Do not settle! You can settle if you want or you can follow the voice within you and never settle for anything or anyone again!"

Imagine, a perfect stranger approaching you in a public place without prior knowledge of who you are. Her approach left me perplexed. What felt like a short time between the words spoken and the reaction, the lady left the nail salon. In utter disbelief, I mustered the courage to ask the lady her name, but didn't get a response. Just like that she was gone. Never to cross paths again.

God had sent me an angel to address me personally and deliver a simple word "Do not settle". It would mark the beginning of my new journey. I'd reached a plateau in life where I was stuck. I'd worked so hard to create an image, but still found myself craving for something, anything that would allow me to feel more fulfilled. The potential inside of me was pushing me towards my purpose in life.

The realization that though I was raised in a Christian home, exposed to revival meetings, prayer and the infilling of the Holy Ghost. That hadn't been enough. There was an absolute need to discover who I was and why I was on this earth.

I began to evaluate my life under the lens of God's word, His perspective and grace. To perceive what God had placed on the inside of me versus what I perceived based on life experiences. I discovered that my destiny was rooted in the love of a father that had gripped me so tightly in his hand. He was not about to drop me or allow me to fail. He was ever-present in all my experiences.

He had chosen me and predestined my adoption before the foundation of the world. Something new would be birthed right there at that nail salon. A desire to pursue my purpose in life while uncovering the potential on the inside of me became more real. There was no doubt that I was made for more.

You see, when you peek through and receive the revelation that something larger-than-life lives on the inside of you, life is never the same again. The potential inside of you includes a blueprint design fashioned by God as the architect. When you understand this blueprint, you recognize the plan which includes your purpose in life. A fresh start beamed so brightly for my life, I endeavored to pursue my purpose with vigor.

Six months before ending a relationship that left me feeling betrayed, I had been afforded another chance in life. I encountered a life-threatening incident one evening while crossing the road to pick up some milk from the store. I became a trauma patient after being hit by a car while crossing the road as a pedestrian. I was tossed in the air, lost consciousness and the memory of the hit. When I came to, paramedics were calling my name as I laid in the middle of the road in an almost fetal position.

My family that witnessed the commotion after the accident said, "It seemed as though someone had picked me up and laid me down on my side with legs curled up." With no broken bones, only contusions to the hips, chest and knees, my life had been spared for a reason. The ER doctor would remind me how "lucky" I was to be alive.

I knew instinctively that God was giving me another chance in life to pursue my purpose, live out my destiny and thrive. One of my favorite quotes describes two moments in life that should be important to each one of us. "The two most important days in your life are the day you are born and the day you find out why." Mark Twain

Do you ever wonder why you're here? Or, how you're supposed

to make a difference in this world? You perceive you're meant to be doing something worthy, something that contributes to society, something that allows you to go to sleep every night feeling good, purposeful, and fulfilled. Ever felt like that?

We've been trained to believe our worth comes from knowing what we are supposed to do. I think this is very hard to figure out when you're young and selecting your college majors and careers. How can you possibly fathom your gifts or how to use them to maximize yourself, or to benefit the world around you?

There are few that can figure this out when they're young, and they chase that purpose for the rest of their lives. My oldest nephew seems to have achieved that level of understanding. It's been a pleasure and a joy to watch him be elevated by God on many levels. Understanding purpose has allowed me to stand in his corner, cheer him on, encourage and support him through this discovery. However, for most of us, it takes living each day, choosing wrong paths, and making wrong decisions to figure out what we're supposed to be doing with our life. We are trained to find careers, and jobs but not our purpose!

Well, amidst the pain of betrayal and feelings of a rug being pulled from underneath me, I uncovered that you cannot judge what is inside of you by what you see on the outside. I had been viewing life based on what was on the inside of me, and the level of my perspective and knowledge was tainted. It was inevitable that I made a 360-degree decision that would bring about complete wholeness; physically, emotionally, mentally and spiritually.

The determination to not settle will push hope inside of you to come alive. Hebrews 11:1 reminds us, *"Now faith is the substance of things hoped for, the evidence of things not seen"* (KJV). Hope is an expected end. When you are highly principled; it's not about the costs, it's about getting to the facts that propel you to an expected end.

It's the knowledge of whose you are and reminding yourself

what Psalm 30:15 says *"weeping may endure for a night, but joy comes in the morning"* (KJV). That it's never too late to start over, get unstuck to live victoriously.

My journey of getting unstuck and the transformation to live out my purpose was not an overnight success. It included several life experiences that would catapult me towards my purpose. I will share in each chapter my personal journey that began with first changing my mind. How I perceived my life had to change. The lens with which I viewed life had to change and the process began with the renewing of my mind.

Even if you must start over, determine in your heart that you will not settle for less than God intended for you. Amid the tears, anguish, and pain, I forged forward. You see the pain was not necessarily the relationships ending or the betrayal. It was the time invested in the families, the memories and the experiences created. My soul (mind, will, and emotions) had been intertwined with these people. I had to untangle myself from the memories and experiences. The journey was real and tough, but worth it.

My greatest lesson was, every conquest has complications and if you wait for the complications to leave, you'll never be a conqueror. You may be quietly questioning God's plan and purpose for your life like I did. Don't let your brokenness get you off the course of transforming your life and discovering why God created you.

I chose to move forward with my wounds still fresh. My pastor used to say, "take a licking and keep on ticking". I purposed that my pain had a purpose, there was greatest hidden on the inside of me and I was willing to endure the dysfunction, uncertainty, frustration and pain. My plan to get unstuck, pursue my purpose and transform my life.

My latter days were greater than my former days. That pain birthed a new company, blogging site, move to another state, building my first home, and living out my purpose. There was more on the inside of me if I was willing to get unstuck. To change my daily routine and focus on positive habits that would drive my purpose and vision in life.

The new lesson learned was, purpose is defined as the reason that something or someone is created or exists. Everywhere we turn we see a flood of authors, speakers, pastors, business leaders, etc. broaching the subject of purpose. I believe God's awakening mankind to go deeper into discovering the meaning of life. To know your purpose is to grasp the reason that God had in mind when He created you, which also gives you the fuel to live up to your fullest potential

"The greatest tragedy in life is not death, but a life without a purpose." - Dr. Myles Munroe. Wouldn't it be a shame if, at the end of your life on earth, you never completed the assignment for which you were created, or discovered the real reason you were chosen to be here on earth from the start? Are you actively, intentionally and purposely pursuing what God has planned and designed for your life?

Realize that discovering your purpose is a process that unfolds day-by-day, and if you are on that journey like a lot of us then you grasp that it takes time, lots of trial and error and is filled with hard lessons along the way. If you want to discover how something works, you go back to inquire of the one who made it. God is the source of life and your existence, so He knows more than anyone what your purpose is. That's what this book is all about.

I will share many nuggets as you prepare for this journey. I hope that they will be valuable, will provoke you to take a moment of quiet introspection, to evaluate where you are stuck and embrace the transformation. I do not apprehend everything about being victorious and living out your purpose, but what I do know I humbly offer you within these pages. These will be word packed nuggets that will empower you to live victorious while grounded in the wisdom and knowledge of God's word.

When you finish the book, you will not only be over the frustrations the past has presented, but you will be in pursuit of the future. You can only conquer your past by focusing on your future. Your victory is not tied to your past or what you'll leave behind, it's tied to a divinely architected plan.

PART 1
Vulnerable Molting

1
Change Your Mind
Shed Plumage

You can change anything, but if you don't change your mind, the same experience in life will perpetuate itself repeatedly because nothing inside changed just outside. There is nothing as powerful as a changed mind. -T. D. Jakes

Anything you focus your mind on, you can change! Life throws curve balls all the time. You can choose to allow life's unexpected spinning to push you away from your destiny or you can decide to change your mind.

You don't always know when people change their mind about you. It just happens! People switch up on you without your knowledge. Have you had people switch up on you suddenly? You thought you had a real friend, a confidant, a shoulder to lean on or a best friend then it all changes one day. We've all experienced at least once in life where a rug was pulled out from underneath us without notice. This is to emphasize that change happens! You can change your mind about anything you focus on.

Change doesn't always have to be referenced to bad experiences. Many times, any change will compel you towards new experiences, new opportunities, it breaks up routines, reveals your strengths, and it will provoke your belief and value systems. Change imparts flexibility, it helps you grow and reminds you to be kind to others.

In this chapter, your focus will be on changing your mind. To change your mind doesn't always equate to an emotional response. It's about a complete 360-degree transformation. I'm referencing a directional change that alters your life, affects your behavior and your future.

This change focuses on transforming yourself, embracing the potential inside of you to pursue your God predestined purpose. You have everything inside of you to change your mind

Every morning, as part of my morning routine, I will brew a cup of tea–Chai Masala. I have become accustomed to this task since I was a young girl growing up in Kenya. I complete this task on default and it requires little thought or effort to brew chai. Chai was and is a daily routine. I remember growing up hearing the older folks say, "anytime is chai time".

We all have tasks that we accomplish on default. Our attitudes, behaviors, and activities like driving are mostly on default. Majority of the time, we hardly put thought on where we are going, and how we got there. Our routines, decisions, and behaviors are on autopilot. We are not actively thinking through a process, a task, behavior or attitude. Many times, our outer actions reflect indifference to inner actions.

You cannot judge anyone by how they act on the outside. They could be smiling at you, with you, but planning your demise secretly. Just because someone is around you all the time with the right attitude does not mean they are on your side. Just because they go to church, doesn't mean they are Christians.

You truly do not know people until you live with them and get to see the reality of who they are. They could be on autopilot (default) in how they behave, express themselves or what they say to you.

Do you often function on default or go about your day on autopilot? How are you managing your attitude and mindset daily? Do you just allow thoughts to run rampage in your mind without actively reviewing what is on your mind? Are you managing your mind and attitude?

You see, life's curve balls can have a major effect on our attitudes, behaviors, and mindsets. Life has taught me that my troubles will either make me better or bitter. We have an opportunity daily to deliberately assess ourselves and what is going on within us . Too often, we do not want to spend time alone reflecting on who we are and why we think the way we think.

You cannot truly begin to change who you are if you do not spend time reviewing your current state. One of the best lessons in life has been to self-regulate. To review my thoughts, ideas, behaviors, and mindset. Let me share the thought-provoking questions that over time have compelled me and continue to challenge my attitudes.

I challenge you to consider incorporating these thought-provoking questions into your life:

- Why do you act the way you do about that person when they walk into the room?
- Do you have an attitude towards other people or are you focusing on pettiness?
- Are you acting according to your core value system?
- Are you ignorant and prideful to situations and people around you?
- Finally, is your attitude corrupting your opportunities at work, relationships with others and the influence you have?

The arrogance of humanity, including you and I, to speak of others' mistakes with the amnesia of our own mistakes is alarming. We are so quick to cast the stone on another person while blindly forgetting our own mistakes. The crisis of being caught in a state of arrogance and ignorance is debilitating and defeating.

You may be asking, Lord, why do I keep going back to the same experiences in life, why do the same type of people seem to recur in my life? Until you change your mind, you will keep going back to the same experiences, hurts, mistakes, and living a life of mediocrity and complacency.

Renewal of my mind was crucial to my transformational journey. The quality decision to change my daily routines, thought-process, and attitude came from the realization that my successful future depended on it. If you change your mind, it doesn't matter what you are dealing with or whom you are fighting. Your life will never the same again.

Romans 12:2 reminds us, *"And be not conformed to this world: but be ye transformed by the renewing of your mind, that ye may prove what is that good, and acceptable, and perfect, will of God,".* It's time to transform your mind! Nothing can defeat you or overwhelm you when you change your mind.

New normal starts with repentance on our deficiency in behaviors, attitudes, habits, and whatever else. Anything you can focus your mind on, you can change. You are the only one who can change the direction of your life. You don't need to be anything that you don't want to be. Be careful with making a permanent decision on temporary situations.

If there is something in my life that I don't like and would like to change, I have the power to change. Acts 17:28 says, *"For, in him, I live and move and have my being."* Let me encourage you today to choose to change your mind on all life's curve balls, emotional garbage, attitudes, habits and anything else you would like to change. You do not have to live in the same situations and circumstances in life.

Read this out loud, I change my mind on how I perceive negative people, how people choose to treat me, I change my mind on how my emotions feel against situations, circumstances, and matters that concern me. I change my mind on the need to be liked or expect others to be there for me. God is there and ever-present. God loves me. He loves me unconditional. He is my Abba Father. I chose to change my mind.

Word Nugget

The word of God is living and has the power to bring change and healing in your life. As you meditate on these scriptures, take inventory and make observations regarding your personal life. Are there any changes that need to be made in your life?

Philippians 4:8 reminds *"Finally, brothers and sisters, whatever is true, whatever is noble, whatever is right, whatever is pure, whatever is lovely, whatever is admirable—if anything is excellent or praiseworthy—think about such things,"*.

Proverbs 23:7 *"As a man thinketh in his heart so is he"*.

2

Forgiveness, an Act of Love
Rejuvenated Talons

When a deep injury is done to us, we never heal until we forgive.
-Nelson Mandela

When we've been hurt by others, we often react as though the individual(s) have taken something from us. We feel that they owe us, yet God wants us to forgive and let go. We've been trained and are accustomed to taking offense and using it as a bargaining chip. The greatest deception that Satan has perpetuated is the idea that if our feelings have not changed, we have not truly forgiven.

Forgiveness does not mean pardon without punishment. It does not exonerate the perpetrator. Forgiveness liberates the victim. It has less to do with what somebody else did as much as it does with your decision to move on with your life and not be continually victimized by rehearsing the issue or incident repeatedly.

Forgiveness is NOT based on being worthy and deserving of it. Forgiveness is an act of grace and mercy. Ultimately, it is an act of LOVE! The art of forgiveness allows the offender to be pardoned, absolved and set free without punishment. It's taking on the nature of God and applying it to the nature of man.

Once you understand that forgiveness is not a white flag of defeat, your perspective changes to something that you want to aspire to. Forgiveness is a big idea. As Bishop T.D. Jakes posits so brilliantly in *Let it Go*, "It takes a person who thinks big ideas rather than comparatively small thoughts to introduce and practice forgiveness effectively."

The ability to achieve forgiveness and let go of past hurts is one of the most critical challenges most of us face in the journey of transformation. Most of us are aggrieved because our emotions have not moved forward. While certainly, it isn't easy. We must get unstuck.

The decision to forgive is an intellectual decision and not an emotional one. The disturbing thing is the notion that we allow our emotions to drive the car and our intellect becomes the passenger. We must ride in the direction of our intellect rather than the other way around.

In *Let it Go*, author Bishop Jakes eloquently reveals, "The reality is, the poison of unquenched anger doesn't infect the perpetrator, but only incarcerates the victim."

In other words, while there is no question that we have the right to feel resentment and the desire to respond accordingly, we can make the choice not to. When we do, we refuse to play the role of the victim and we let go of the control and power that the offending person, or situation, has over us. We choose to not allow grudges, hurt or wrongdoings to define our lives.

Forgiveness simply releases the debt they owe you so that God can release the debt you owe Him. "For if ye forgive men their trespasses, your heavenly Father will also forgive you: But if ye forgive not men their trespasses, neither will your Father forgive your trespasses," (Matthew 6:14-15 KJV).

Sometimes in reading these verses, people get the wrong idea about God. They think He's mad because they've failed to forgive someone and as a means of punishment, He is withholding His forgiveness from them. But, that's not the case. God wants to forgive all of us, all the time, for everything. That's why He sent Jesus to the cross. So, there's never a time when He is unwilling to forgive us.

To forgive others, we must be willing to look at our ability to hurt, offend, and injure those around us, often the people we love the most. When you decide to forgive someone, it becomes part of transforming your mind. Don't let the devil convince you that because you still have feelings that you've not forgiven the person, that forgiveness has not taken place.

You can decide to forgive and not feel differently. That's when faith steps in. You have done your part, now wait on God. He will do His part and heal your emotions, make you whole, and change your feelings toward the person who hurt you.

"We think that forgiveness is a weakness, but it's absolutely not; it takes a very strong person to forgive," -T. D. Jakes

Time itself does not perform the healing. A passage of time allows the mind to process the trauma and move through shock and disbelief, grief, rage, insecurity, guilt, shame, and blame. It's important to figure out who has hurt you and how. This may seem obvious, but not every action that causes you suffering is unjust. For example, you don't need to forgive your child or your spouse for being imperfect, even if their imperfections are inconvenient for you.

However, healing is an active conscious process, which can only occur when you allow God to restore your soul. It's time spent reading and meditating on what the word of God says about forgiveness. People who don't heal traumatic hurts through forgiveness can carry festering wounds for a lifetime.

We must find meaning in what we have endured. Without meaning, you can lose a sense of purpose, which can lead to hopelessness and a despairing conclusion that there is no meaning to life itself. That doesn't mean we look for suffering to grow or try to find goodness in another's bad actions. Instead, we try to see how our suffering has changed us positively.

Jesus taught that forgiveness is an ongoing process. Jesus answered, I tell you, not seven times, but seventy-seven times (Matthew 18:22 NIV). Jesus instructs us to forgive the same offense over and over. It also means forgiving a multitude of offenses that come our way every day, from family members, friends, church members, coworkers, and strangers.

Not only is unforgiveness a violation of love, but it's also one of the costliest sins we can commit. I am fully convinced that if believers understood just how deadly the consequences can be, they would never, ever fail to quickly and freely forgive.

"Therefore, I tell you, whatever you ask for in prayer, believe that you have received it, and it will be yours. And when you stand praying, if you hold anything against anyone, forgive them, so that your Father in heaven may forgive you your sins" (Mark 11:24-26 NIV).

When you hold on to unforgiveness, you hinder your faith, growth in Christ and stop your prayers from being answered. You open the door to sickness and disease while closing the door to healing. Some people have suffered terrible illnesses, all the while calling on God for help. Yet, because they continue to cling on bitterness and resentment, refusing to forgive someone who hurt them, they are unable to receive the healing they so desperately need.

Unforgiveness cosigns us to a life of guilt and condemnation because it stops us from receiving the sense of forgiveness from God that we need to be restored. When we sin and need forgiveness from him, our refusal to forgive another will make it seem the heavens are brass and the door to God's throne rooms has been closed to us.

It's no wonder that, in the sight of God, forgiveness is such a serious business. He knows that if we refuse to forgive, we'll become prisoners of failure and defeat. Don't let the enemy deceive you that some offenses you carry are too small to cause you any harm. After all, it's just a little unforgiveness, a minor grudge. In the great, big scheme of things, it won't make much difference.

Forgiveness, an Act of Love

On the other hand, the enemy will convince you that the major mistreatment you suffered cannot be dismissed. It was too painful and too costly. Surely God himself must understand that until you see justice done, you can't let it go. The devil is a liar.

Jesus' words remain unmistakably clear "If you hold anything against anyone, forgive." Anything and anyone. Amid my pain, hurt, betrayal and rejection. I learned to reach out to God and ask Him to search my heart. It is there where I opened myself for him to show me the level of unforgiveness that was blocking me from receiving His love and blessing.

Ask Him to show you more about this gift of forgiveness so that you can walk in his freedom and victory. God has a comprehensive policy on forgiveness. When you abide by it, it will protect you from unnecessary pain and keep you in the place of answered prayer.

Forgiveness is about emancipating yourself rather than empowering your past. Forgiveness has unshackled me to focus on my purpose rather than hold on to the past. Forgiveness is founded on love, and it is the most powerful weapon that anyone can possess.

Forgiveness is taking the knife out your own back and not using it to hurt anyone else. No matter how they hurt you. We have to focus on walking out of what incarcerates us and the trauma of the hurt. Jesus' teachings focused on forgiveness. He gave humanity the greatest gift of forgiveness. When we've received divine forgiveness for ourselves, forgiving others becomes mandatory. If we are walking in God's grace, forgiveness flows from a spirit of humility and awareness of our shortcomings.

Forgiveness is about extending grace. You put that grace before other emotions because grace is much more important. It means gracefully letting things go that are not meant for you. It means going beyond your inclinations of trying to get the upper hand or revenge on someone who hurt you. It's about receiving the apology that you never got. To forgive them even if they were not sorry.

In the process of forgiveness, you will lose many things from the past, but you will find yourself. Forgiveness doesn't excuse their behavior. It prevents their behavior from destroying your soul. It's a gift you give yourself.

> *"It's one of the greatest gifts you can give yourself, to forgive. Forgive everybody," -Maya Angelou*

Word Nugget

The bible is the word of God. It is life and has the power to bring change and healing in your life. It is designed to nourish the soul and spirit in the same way food nourishes the body. As you meditate on the scriptures, take inventory and any observations regarding your personal life.

Colossians 3:13 Bear with each other and forgive one another if any of you has a grievance against someone. Forgive as the Lord forgave you

Food for Thought

The word of God is full of wisdom and guidance on forgiveness. Seek the Lord on how to deal with any unforgiveness in your life. Any small ounce of unforgiveness will cancel God's blessings from being received in your life.

The first step to forgiveness is the decision to forgive. You must decide to let go and let God. Once you've made the decision, then you PRAY about your decision, asking God to help you, knowing that you have no power of your own to do so.

3

Get Unstuck
Rise Above Challenges and Seasonal Changes

The first step towards getting somewhere is to decide that you are not going to stay where you are.
-Unknown

I don't have to explain that we live in a stressful world. Our modern and technologically advanced world has made us surrender to the simplicity of life. We are moving at a faster pace due to our modern gadgets. We are taking on more responsibilities, attempting to squeeze activities into a typical day.

So, increased stressed is an unintended consequence of our technology crazed life. The ever-changing daily bustle doesn't allow us to stop and consider our lifeblood; what's on the inside of us. Very few people have the convenience of locking themselves away from society.

Life can have you so caught up that you do not have time to uncover the potential on the inside of you. To better understand what is at the core of who you are and how to get unstuck, you must transform your thinking to align with the word of God. Your understanding of what the word says about you brings about the revelation to uncover your potential and pursue God's purpose for your life

So, what is at the core of who you are? Do you know who you are? Have you taken the time to uncover the potential on the inside of you?

When you know you are a child of God with a great future, created with the potential for a purpose. You are aware of what his word says, that you can do all things through Christ who strengthens you Philippians 4:13 NKJV. Even with the knowledge of the word of God; there are times when you still think like you've come short of answering these questions. These truths should encourage you, however instead you find yourself further from understanding the potential on the inside for the specific purpose in life.

The first step to getting unstuck is finding the freedom to fully embrace yourself as you are and not compare yourself to anyone or anything. You are not wired to be anyone else but yourself. You do not want to spend the rest of your life being something, someone you were not created to be. You must rise above the opinions of others, reach beyond the expectations of others. God created us in his image to our uniqueness. He predestined us before the foundation of the world.

Jeremiah 29:11 reminds us, "For I know the plans I have for you, declares the Lord, plans for welfare and not for evil, to give you a future and a hope" (ESV). You are in a class all by yourself. You are to work from the potential inside, what God put inside of you. When you embody what's on the inside, outwardly working off what's internal, you open doors to getting unstuck.

Paul reminds us in Romans 12:2: "And be not conformed to this world: but be ye transformed by the renewing of your mind (emphasis added), that ye may prove what is that good, and acceptable, and perfect, will of God" (KJV). The word Paul uses here is the word we use for the metamorphosis of a butterfly. The change, in the end, is something completely different from what was there before.

This is how complete the transformation should be when it comes to our thoughts. Remember, our thoughts determine our actions. Be willing to be changed and not to be manipulated. Your goal is to be the highest presentation of whom God created you to be.

It's very important for you to not allow people to mold you; to be what they need you to be just because they need it. You do not allow people to mold you based on their void. You do not shape your life based on other people's experiences, prophecies or inclinations. We are used to being told who we should be. It's time to have a different perspective.

Second, it is essential that each person take time to withdraw from the constant bombardment of life's pressures and simply seek a place of solace and celebrate their uniqueness. You are not indestructible. God didn't intend for you to carry these many loads in a given day.

One of the greatest things about life is also the worst thing about life. Life is a series of choices, but with every choice, there is a resulting consequence. And that is where life gets complicated. You must refuse to allow external forces or experiences to manipulate and control you from unearthing hidden treasures within you. So, take some time to spoil yourself and to validate your own needs.

When you carve out time to discover your hidden treasures, your life is bound to change. You become who God made you to be. You uncover God's best plans for you. You unwrap better ways to improve your finances and relationships. You boost your creativity and your blessings come.

You must determine to get unstuck, so you can find the purpose in your life. Not finding your purpose, can be likened to a driver who gets in a car and goes in circles and says, "I am driving". When one drives a car, there is a purpose and destination in mind. Stop driving in circles. If you've lost yourself, get back to your core and find out who you are supposed to be. When in doubt, go back to your origin?

If you want to rekindle anything or revive anything in life, going back to your essence is key. The power is in your essence. You cannot withdraw from a bank account what you have never deposited into that account. Likewise, you can never withdraw from life what you have never deposited into life. Be ye transformed by the renewing of your mind. Do not allow what happened to you to control what's left of you. Whatever is on the inside of you may be laying dormant awaiting your discovery.

Your life depends on what is inside of you. You will never be what you were meant to be if you keep allowing external forces to influence you. Your frustration is that you have too much inside of you to allow it to rot away like you are allowing. You must be transformed by the renewing of your mind.

Until you find your essence, you will never find your future and you will remain stuck. Start investing your time into your purpose and possibilities. At the core, what do you care about? What gets on your nerves?

We are most passionate about changing things we care about. We have been trained to believe that other people need to do something about what we care about. Well, that person you are waiting for is YOU! You have the power to change what you are concerned about, the power to get unstuck is inside of you. Anything that concerns you, you can change!

Word Nugget

The word of God is designed to nourish the soul and spirit in the same way food nourishes the body. Inventory your life and honestly evaluate every area of your life. Take time to renew your mind, prepare for action and reach forth for what God has set before you.

1 Peter 1:13 reminds us *"Therefore, preparing your minds for action, and being sober-minded, set your hope fully on the grace that will be brought to you at the revelation of Jesus Christ,"* (ESV).

Be what God sees in you! Let Him transform you so you can be free. It's time to get unstuck.

Food for Thought

What truly concerns you? Where are you stuck emotionally, spiritually and physically? How does a transformed life look like for you? Do you need to renew your mind about anything? Are you moving through life on default and staying stuck? Have you made your comfort zone around your dysfunction?

PART 2
Emerge Sharper & Stronger

4

God Chose You
Powerful Vision and Revelation

Long before the enemy targeted you, God chose you.
-Lisa Bevere

To consistently experience a victorious life. You must understand that there is a price tag associated with every decision you make. It is easy to buy into too many things that life dangles in front of you. Your victory hinges on you uncovering the treasures within and understanding God's purpose for your life.

To thrive and live a fulfilled life, it's important to discover why God created you and grasp the knowledge that He chose you. You must learn to focus on the few things that matter to you and pour yourself into those important things while rejecting all the other distractions of life.

The truth is God chose you for His purpose and His perfect will. We've all been born with a deep and meaningful purpose. Your purpose is not something you need to makeup; it's already there. Knowing and finding your purpose will propel you towards living a victorious life.

Ephesians 1:3-6 exhorts us, "*Blessed be the God and Father of our Lord Jesus Christ, who has blessed us with every spiritual blessing in the heavenly places in Christ, just as **He chose us** in Him before the foundation of the world, that we should be holy and without blame* *before Him in love, having predestined us to adoption as sons by Jesus Christ to Himself, according to the good pleasure of His will, to the praise of the glory of His grace, by which He has made us accepted in the Beloved,"* (NIV).

Believing you are chosen by God is an important part of our faith. More importantly, that God who has called us is mighty to accomplish the work He has begun in us. God has not called any of us at random. It was predestined before the foundation of the world and made possible by grace in Jesus Christ, through His life, death, and resurrection.

His plan and purpose for our lives were predestined according to the good pleasure of His will. He accepts you and me as beloved. We cannot begin to understand God. When you imagine all His attributes; His power, eternal being, omnipresence, omnipotent, love, holiness and much more. It is unfathomable to try to fit God in our limited imagination. So why would you doubt his plan for your life?

The word reminds us that we are to praise God the Father for the blessing that is already ours. We have the assurance and certainty from the father that the heavenly resources are always there for us. We are to have an attitude of praise because everything we need or will ever need to be victorious has been provided.

He has blessed us with *every spiritual blessing*. Everything we need to unleash our potential and pursue our purpose has been provided. Every blessing we receive, we receive it in Christ. You name it, He has given it to us. God wants to bless us. He withholds nothing good from us. This has always been in the plan and purpose of God.

Our possession of every spiritual blessing to live a fulfilled and victorious life is as certain as our being *chosen in Him* before *the foundation of the world*. We were chosen by God before we had done anything or become anything. This revelation of God's selection assures us to the permanence of His plan and His love towards us.

The reasons for God's choices are not capricious, nor are they random. Though they are past our human understanding, we know that they are altogether wise and good. All the reasons are all in Him, not in us. His choosing is according to the good pleasure of His will.

We are chosen for holiness and blamelessness in love. Understanding that God chooses us diminishes our responsibility for personal holiness and sanctification, which falls far short of the whole counsel of God. This is the assurance that no matter how you feel inside, or the uncertainties life throws at you, God has a plan for you. You are victorious and guaranteed to win in every aspect of your life.

God chose us to be used by Him exactly according to His perfect plan. He laid out a clear path for us to walk on. Despite our fears and doubts, we each have a great role set before us and wonderful things to accomplish for the Kingdom. He chose us before the foundation of the world for his perfect will.

God formed us and gave His power perfectly to us to grasp the amazing potential within us. But we must trust Him more than we trust our own eyes to seize daily victories. We may get discouraged and wish that God called someone else, but that is the flesh talking. We should resist any subtle resistances to God's plan and purpose for our lives.

While you should always strive to be holy, you cannot be anyone else other than you and that is just perfect for the purpose God has for you. As you continue to unveil your potential and purpose, renewing your mind should be a daily endeavor. Settle in the knowledge that you are rooted in God's plan; not what your external environment has deceived you to believe. Confidence and trust in God's purpose for your life will elevate you towards the path of victory in every area of your life.

Word Nugget

The word of God is designed to nourish the soul and spirit in the same way food nourishes the body. Inventory your life and honestly evaluate your belief system on God's creation plan for you?

Ephesians 2:10 *"For we are God's masterpiece. He has created us anew in Christ Jesus, so we can do the good things he planned for us long ago."*

Determine to remain rooted in God's plan for your life. Ascertain to daily renew your mind in the WORD of God regarding his love for you. Be grounded in the knowledge that God is working in you. He is giving you the desire and power to do what pleases him. He chose you, and that's final!

Philippians 2:13 *"For God is working in you, giving you the desire and the power to do what pleases him."*

5

Identity in Christ
Your Transformation is Solidified

Saturate your mind with the truth of God's Word. It is filled with reminders of His unconditional love for you!
-Joyce Meyer

As you uncover your potential, there is a need to establish your identity. Do you know your identity? Our identity, how we see ourselves is often shaped by our early experiences in life. No matter what your childhood experiences were, there is life-changing truth when you discover your identity in Christ.

If we're honest with ourselves, we often express insecurity. Those who hide it best often feel it most, but our insecurity is an invitation from God to escape the danger of false beliefs about who we are and find true peace in who He is.

At the heart of what it means to be a Christian is to receive a new identity. In Jesus, we do not lose our true selves, but we become our true selves, only in him. What does it mean to have your identity in Christ? 2 Corinthians 5:17 says, "Therefore, if anyone is in Christ, he is a new creation, the old has gone, the new has come" (NIV).

Christ in you, what does that mean? Christ is our life — not only the guarantee of it in heaven but the down payment of it by the

Spirit now, as he lives in us. His joy becomes our joy; his love, our love; his peace, our peace; his strength, our strength. We became new beings; all the odd stuff passed away (the old dead and now alive in Christ). Remember, first you are a spirit who possesses a soul and lives in a physical body.

One of the most important revelations we can receive from the word of God is to understand our identity in Christ. Identity in Christ will change the way you live and will always cause you to rise above adversity. It ignites a fire on the inside of you to live according to your rights and privileges in Christ. Everything that Christ is, you are.

Christ in you, means that you identify with Christ. In our everyday lives, we are always identifying with a person, nationality, organization, church or occupation. We also have the same in our spiritual realm, Paul wrote to remind us "To whom God would make known what is the riches of the glory of this mystery among the Gentiles; which is Christ in you, the hope of glory" (Colossians 1:27 KJV)? Christ in you the hope of glory (manifested).

You are hidden and rooted in Christ. When your focus becomes "Christ in you", then you are made perfect because He is perfect. All your answers are in Christ, your focus should be on Christ. When we understand our identity in Christ, who we are in Him, it changes the way we think and live.

If we are distracted from who we are, then we can be distracted from what we have, the potential and purpose in our lives. The devil doesn't want you to discover what you have, which is you are predestined to win because you are in Christ. You are an expression of the life of Christ because He is in your life. You have been made complete in Christ. This is only possible when you are in Christ.

When we become self-occupied, we are full of fear, panic, stress, pain, and trouble. It's self-centeredness - it's the root of all bitterness and unforgiveness. When you are in the center, it will bother you when people talk about you. It will bother you when people exclude you. It shouldn't bother you when you are not in the center. You, at your core, should be solidified by your relationship in Christ.

We are reminded, "Therefore, as you received Christ Jesus the Lord, so walk in him, rooted and built up in him and established in the faith, just as you were taught, abounding in thanksgiving" (Colossians 2:6-7 ESV). When you are Christ occupied, you are joyful, peaceful, and full of life. When trouble brews, walk around confessing that you are in Christ because you are firmly rooted and built up in him.

So, when you are in Christ, everything about you is mirrored in Christ. How do I manifest all that I am in Christ? By believing with my heart and confessing with my mouth. Christ in me gives me access to all these things. By relentlessly pursuing and becoming who God says I am.

I've discovered that if I want to see the reflection on whom I look like in Christ, I am to open the word of God. Confession is admitting and acknowledging; by acknowledging everything in me is in Christ. When I confess it, the manifestation in my life is visible. The confession I hold fast to is *Christ in me*, brings the reality of all that I am in Christ.

Word Nugget

The word of God is designed to nourish the soul and spirit in the same way food nourishes the body. Pause and inventory your life and honestly evaluate the areas in which you are struggling.

Take time to recite these scriptures, confess them over and over until you become one with them.

"Faith confessions create realities," -Creflo Dollar

You are a new creature (2 Cor. 5:17).
You are the righteousness of God (2 Cor. 5:21).
You've been healed (1 Peter 2:24).
You've been made rich (2 Cor. 8:9).
You are accepted (Eph. 1:6).
You are free from sin (Rom. 6:20-22)

Food for Thought

I challenge you today to value Christ and His word. Heb 4:14 says, "Therefore, since we have a great high priest who has gone through the heavens, Jesus the Son of God, let us hold firmly to the faith we profess." What God says about you is found in His Word. Who you are in Christ must take root into the core of who you. God has the final word!

This has been a GREAT lesson worth practicing daily in my life. I have seen wonderful changes in my life by understanding my identity in Christ. You won't want to go back once you start. Journey with me as you continue to uncover a victorious life. A life no longer stuck, embracing your potential in Christ.

6
Uncover Your Potential
Significance and Relevance of Your Wings

The big challenge is to become all that you have the possibility of becoming. You cannot believe what it does to the human spirit to maximize your human potential and stretch yourself to the limit.
-Jim Rohn

Let's consider an apple... Most of us eat the apple and throw away the most important part of the apple–the core. When you bite into an apple, you don't notice the core immediately. The core–the middle part of an apple that consists of seeds. These seeds produce real apple fruit. So, what is at your core? What's hidden on the inside of you?

How do you see yourself? How do you digest and recognize what is going on inside and outside you? Are you embracing what you need to be learning about you?

To truly learn, recognize and digest what is going on with you. You need to grasp the truth that potential lives on the inside of you. You are authentic, whatever God put inside of you is solid. That's where your creativity comes from, your authenticity and passion draw from that source.

Gen 1:11 reminds us *"And God said, Let the earth bring forth grass, the herb yielding seed, and the fruit tree yielding fruit after his kind, whose seed is in itself, upon the earth: and it was so"* (KJV). You have everything on the inside of you. Before creation, God predestined so much on the inside of each of us. What we need to be creative and more is on the inside of us.

You won't need to imitate others or be intimidated by people around you when you learn to be happy with yourself. Once you uncover who you are, learn to celebrate yourself, and embrace who you are in a class all by yourself. Nobody can be you no matter how good or smart they are. You begin to change how you relate to yourself. Your focus is redirected, and a new perspective dawns in your life.

My experience, through the journey to uncover potential, was empowering. I quickly discovered that I cannot have relationships if I don't know how to relate to myself. To relate to others doesn't mean comparing oneself to others.

It's wholeheartedly, accepting who I am and all about me. It takes courage, empathy, acceptance, and kindness to oneself. It's about making a demand from the core of who I am. Uncovering how to stand up and face who I am and why I move the way I do was explosive to embracing the uniqueness within.

We are all unique and different, we do not need to be jealous of each other. When you learn and discover what is at your core, you begin to make demand out of it. The new mindset, the new thought-process, the new default inside of your core needs to be protected.

You must make sure you do not fall back to the old default that you used to be. To make sure you are performing from your new place, you need to make a demand from your core. Stop looking horizontally unto others but vertically to God.

The Psalmist reminds us, *"Those who look to him are radiant; their faces are never covered with shame"* (Psalm 34:5 ESV). Key is to embrace who you are from the inside out. His radiance is upon those who look unto him. Your radiance comes from what God placed on the inside of you.

When you uncover your potential, it allows you to detach from all the spinning and changes of life. Life is going to continue changing. If you are waiting for it to stop. You will never be secured by the outer perimeter of the external forces that keep spinning. You will not be stable enough to start anything in life if you are expecting life to slow down or stop moving.

In a world of constant movement, you need to find your core. Stop allowing what is going on around you to direct you. Although things are constantly moving and changing, you will do best to detach yourself from all of the external movement. When you are anchored within, you will find that you can remain steadfast, unmovable, abounding in the work of the Lord. Drawing strength from your inner man.

What are you anxious about? Philippians exhorts us, *"Do not be anxious about anything, but in every situation, by prayer and petition, with thanksgiving, present your requests to God. And the peace of God, which transcends all understanding, will guard your hearts and your minds in Christ Jesus. Finally, brothers and sisters, whatever is true, whatever is noble, whatever is right, whatever is pure, whatever is lovely, whatever is admirable if anything is excellent or praiseworthy think about such things,"* (Philippians 4:6-8 NIV).

When you take your hands off the ever-changing and movement of life (who left you, what was said about you, who hated you, why you are unsatisfied with your present state, who criticized you, who doesn't love you, who doesn't respect you, who doesn't think you are cute) all this stuff will change next month.

Permit yourself to anchor in whom God created you to be! You can withstand the storms and uncertainties of life, it won't be long, soon you will anchor again. Your greatness, power, authenticity, and creativity are in you. Step back and embrace your potential. Do you!

It takes courage to confront your idols (the things you have in mind because of whom you spend time with, what happened to you, the experiences in life and your coping mechanism). Focus on who you are and avoid overindulging into other people's lives. If you do not change how you process life, you will not be able to change the progress in life. It all begins with the uncovering who you are and unleashing the potential on the inside.

If you're going to have any virtue, excellence or praiseworthy in your life, it's a direct derivative of what you think. Proverbs 23:7 says, *"For as he thinketh in his heart, so is he"* (KJV). Your thinking will change or destroy your life. Is your attitude defeating to your altitude?

As you begin to seek God for clarity and wisdom, begin looking into your life. Is there a specific cycle of things that keep happening to you? If you are going to break the cycle, you will need to uncover what's in your core and stabilize your life at the center by embracing your potential.

Look at your life, 20 years later are you having the same experiences with different names? All people are leaving you, clinging to you or abusing you or using you. Are the names changing and the relationships the same? Be ye transformed by the renewing of your mind.

You cannot let the old you make decisions anymore, the new you must make demands from your core. Be conscious of protecting your core. The only way to protect the core is to produce from the core. You must make sure you do not go back to who you used to be. The only way I can make sure I do not go back to who I used to be is I make a demand to produce from my core.

The core holds the seeds, and the seeds hold the next best version of who you are. But you cannot expect to harvest from somewhere you did not water. You need to produce from the core, the new mindset, the new spirituality. You realize that you have a destiny, sometimes your destiny and core are not in alignment. If you are not careful, you can bring your default setting and sabotage your destiny. Your core needs to align with what God placed on the inside of you.

As I embraced my core and anchored myself in God. I found joy and peace that He placed on the inside of me. I began celebrating and loving who I am, I did not need validation from people because he already confirmed me. I relied upon his guidance through life's ferociousness as he quieted me in His presence. I prayed "God if you can change what's on the inside of me and reveal it, you can change the outside and what I'm surrounded by".

The psalmist wrote "You make known to me the path of life; in your presence, there is the fullness of joy; at your right hand are pleasures forevermore," (Psalm 16:11 ESV).

So, when what begins on the inside of you moves to your lips and comes out of your mouth becomes tangible for everyone to see will eventually begin to attract questions. That's when you know that you are producing from your core. Your hidden treasures begin to attract questions from others, a sign you are uncovering your potential. The questions about, where did this talent come from, who did you know and how did you get there? The constant questions provoked me to remain hidden in the Lord.

He knows my secrets, the things that are right inside of me. He guides me towards the untouched gifts and treasures on the inside of me. It is in my creator that I find why I move as I do, and why I am shaped as I am. It's because I am his child.

Acts 17:28 reminds us, *"For in him we live and move and have our being. As some of your poets have said, 'We are his offspring"* (NIV). And for that reason, I chose to remain anchored and hidden in him, so my full potential may be realized. Choose to uncover your potential, to unleash the treasure on the inside.

Word Nugget

The bible is the word of God. It is life and has the power to bring change and healing in your life. The word of God is designed to nourish the soul and spirit in the same way food nourishes the body. Spend some time reading the scriptures, read out loud and memorize, if possible.

Psalm 139: 13-16 *"For you formed my inward parts; you knitted me together in my mother's womb. I praise you, for I am fearfully and wonderfully made. Wonderful are your works; my soul knows it very well. My frame was not hidden from you, when I was being made in secret, intricately woven in the depths of the earth. Your eyes saw my unformed substance; in your book were written, every one of them, the days that were formed for me, when yet there was none of them."*

Food for Thought

As you meditate on the scriptures, take inventory, consider these thoughts and any observations regarding your personal life. Have you lost sight of who God created you to be and what he designed you to be? Are you actively, intentionally and purposely pursuing what God has planned and designed for your life?

You will have to face up to these truths:

1. God has placed more on the inside of you than you realize.
2. You have likely settled for the life you live now.

PART 3

The Wind and Your Wings

Pursue Your Purpose
Spread Your Wings, You Have A Bigger Purpose

The deepest craving of the human spirit is to find a sense of significance and relevance. The search for relevance in life is the ultimate pursuit of man.
-Dr. Myles Munroe

To wake up with a sense of no purpose is incredibly frustrating. You look around and see your friends and coworkers living passionate, engaged, meaningful lives. They have deep relationships, rewarding jobs and a sense of direction that compels them to hop out of bed each morning with a spring in their step

Purpose is the reason that something or someone is created or exists. It is the only source of individual and corporate fulfillment. Everywhere we turn we can see a flood of authors, speakers, pastors, business leaders, etc. broaching the subject of purpose. I believe God's awakening mankind to go deeper into discovering the meaning of life.

To know your purpose is to know the reason that God had in mind when He created you, which also gives you the fuel to live up to your fullest potential. It's the key to life. Without purpose, life has no meaning.

You know that God has something good in store for you. You

don't believe he intends for you to live a life of painful drudgery in which each day is a total drag. Millions are busy making a living, but they experience very little of life. Without purpose, life becomes a string of activities with little or no significance.

Know that discovering your purpose is a process that unfolds day-by-day, and if you are on that journey like a lot of us then you realize that it takes time, lots of trial and error and is filled with hard lessons along the way. If you want to discover how something works, you go back to inquire of the one who made it. God is the source of life and your existence, so He knows more than anyone what your purpose is.

> *"The greatest tragedy in life is not death, but life without a reason. It is dangerous to be alive and not know why you were given life"*
> *- Dr. Myles Munroe.*

One of the most frustrating experiences is to have time but not know why. Wouldn't it be a shame if at the end of your life on earth that you never completed the assignment for which you were created, or discovered the real reason you were chosen to be here on earth to start?

Before we dive into this point, we need to make at least one caveat. In one sense, you are always living in God's purpose. God is God, and He works all things, including your life, according to his purposes. Nothing can happen without God ordaining it.

Psalm 57:2 says, *"I cry out to God Most High, to God who fulfills his purpose for me."* This is key to understanding God's purpose for your life. God has numbered your days and will fulfill every purpose He has for you.

However, our choices and actions also really matter. In some ways, this is a mystery we can't fully understand, but that doesn't mean it's not true. We can choose to do things that will bring us more joy and give us more of a sense of purpose.

In Pursuit of Purpose, Dr. Myles Munroe's book, he brilliantly writes, "Purpose is the master of motivation and the mother of commitment. It is the source of enthusiasm and the womb of perseverance. Purpose gives birth to hope and instills the passion to act. It is the common denominator that gives every creature an element of distinction. This guiding sense of purpose is more than an orientation toward a goal".

To Identify that passion can bring more excitement into the God-given purpose in your life. Purpose is an intense awareness that encompasses life and existence. Without purpose, we only exist. We sense no passion for a living, neither do we have a reason to wake up in the morning.

We must realize that anytime we feel purposeless, it's because we haven't grasped the full meaning of our life. You see, our fulfillment in life is dependent on discovering who we are and working towards the goal of accomplishing what we were created to do. Unless we discover our purpose, our existence has no meaning, because purpose is the source of fulfillment.

There are ways to regain that powerful awareness and pursue your purpose. Only God knows the purpose for your life. He created you with a purpose in mind. He is a great architect with the blueprint for your life. You can ask God to give you wisdom and direction. James 1:5 states, *"If any of you lacks wisdom, let him ask God, who gives generously to all without reproach, and it will be given him."* That's incredibly good news.

God wants to give you a purpose. He wants to bestow divine wisdom on you. It's not like God is holding out on you to make you miserable. He desires you to have a joyful, ambitious, purposeful life. Ask God for purpose and expect Him to give it to you.

God is a God of purpose. He is an intentional God. He created everything with a specific purpose in place. Even the rodents we so detest when we find out they are infesting our attics. Even they were created for a specific purpose. Everything, no matter how insignificant it may seem, exists for a distinct purpose in the mind of God to serve a greater purpose.

Another thing you should do in your search for God's purpose is to start digging into scripture. Now, you won't find any verses that tell you to become a writer or an engineer, but you will begin to understand the heart of God.

Psalm 119:105 says, *"Your word is a lamp to my feet and a light to my path."* God's word brings light to paths that otherwise seem dark. In the Bible, you learn how to live wisely in God's world, which is the first step toward finding your purpose.

God has given you very specific gifts and strengths. Maybe you're an entrepreneur or a genius music writer. Maybe you have a mind for computers or business. You could be great at organizing people and getting things done. God's purpose for you probably involves the things you're already good at.

What is one thing you're particularly passionate about? It can be anything; business, art, economics, alleviating poverty or empowering others. If money wasn't an issue, what would you enjoy doing today? Being certain about your passions often helps you figure out what God has called you to do. It's often said that God works at the intersection of our gifts and our passions. Where do your gifts meet your passions?

Sometimes it can be incredibly helpful to get away from it all and take some solitude time to think, pray and journal. You don't have to spend a week in the woods for this to be effective. Even just a day away from the hustle and bustle can be greatly rewarding.

During these moments of retreat, allow yourself to be still. To ponder. To ask God for direction and listen for His voice. This doesn't need to be complicated and doesn't require any elaborate rituals. Hebrews 11:6 is a reminder that God always rewards those who seek him. He's not too busy to listen or trying to keep his will hidden from you. He wants to guide you.

Your purpose determines your potential, which determines the demands made on you by the One who made you. Knowing your purpose is the key to using your potential because once you discover your purpose in life you can also learn how much potential God stored inside you to meet the demands He would make on you.

If you don't know your purpose, you will probably live below your potential. Potential is equal to purpose.

Word Nugget

The bible is the word of God. It is life and has the power to bring change and healing in your life. The word of God is designed to nourish the soul and spirit in the same way food nourishes the body.

Spend some time reading the scriptures, read out loud and memorize, if possible.

Psalm 16:11 *"You will show me the way of life, granting me the joy of your presence and the pleasures of living with you forever."*

Jeremiah 29:11 *"I know the plans I have for you, says the Lord. 'They are the plan for good and not for disaster, to give you a future and a hope".*

Colossians 1:16 *"For in him all things were created: things in heaven and on earth, visible and invisible, whether thrones or powers or rulers or authorities; all things have been created through him and for him."*

Food for Thought

As you meditate on the scriptures, take inventory and any observations regarding your personal life. Are you pursuing the plan and purpose God has for you? Does your life reflect what the word of God says about his plan for you?

8

Settle in His Presence
Conserve Your Energy, Use the Wind

The presence of God will not always fix your problems, but it will clarify your perspective.
-Steve Furtick

Our daily lives are entangled in a web of hustle and bustle. Many of us are caught up solving issues, situations, and circumstances that bombard us. We operate on autopilot with no clear direction or purpose. We remain focused on what's in front of us.

Our goals become to go to work and take care of family or life's responsibilities. We hardly take the time to stop and soak our day. No opportunity to pause to enjoy or celebrate our lives or recognize the surrounding relationships. Most of us don't stop during the day to connect with our spiritual side. Neither do we spend time considering how is it that I'm breathing, moving and have more than enough. Who is responsible for all of it? Who made it possible for me to deserve it all?

We find ourselves so engulfed in our lives, that most of our concerns become self-centered. We are worried about what we will eat, why so and so is not communicating with us. We begin to base our self-worth on what we do for a living, who we are in a relationship with, and the friendships we are connected to. We are focused on us and hardly ever stop to consider our spiritual relationship with God or how to be a blessing to another person.

When we experience a breakdown in communication, reciprocation with loved ones or friends there is a tendency to reflect on the lack of reciprocation and fall back to the default setting that we must have done something wrong. We ask the questions, what did we do wrong? How come the relationship changed? What contributing factors did we play to fuel the lack of communication or reciprocation?

The truth is most of the breakdown has nothing to do with you. It's all centered around the other individual life's circumstances and situations currently engulfing, and entangling them with no chance to look up, let alone think of another person. The same applies to you and me. We hardly make time for anyone.

The majority of us become distracted and preoccupied with solving problems in our lives. We forget to reciprocate, reach out, or follow through with plans previously made with loved ones or friends. Other times, we might not consider a relationship as a priority in our lives. At times, we are overwhelmed with agendas that mean something to us.

One of the best lessons I've learned is that no matter how preoccupied or distant people become, you cannot base your self-worth on people, what they do or don't do, say or don't say or even what they may imply. Whether people reach back when they say they would or if they never follow through, what they do or don't do should never affect how we perceive ourselves.

Their actions are not a reflection of who you are or your self-worth. It's a reflection of who they are. We must be strong enough to walk away from unproductive relationships and those that no longer serve us. Lack of reciprocation or communication should no longer distract us from living victoriously. Let that soak in, stop holding yourself responsible for every broken relationship, instead determine to find the kind of relationships that nourish and support you.

Your perspective and self-worth need to be deeply rooted

in God's word. His description of you is wonderful, fearfully made, highly favored, loved, and treasured. He sees you as capable, confident, and a conqueror. No matter where you are or even amid broken relationships, weariness or loneliness. Let God be your rest. Philippians 4:7 says *"And the peace of God, which transcends all understanding, will guard your hearts and your minds in Christ Jesus."*

Let me share the truth I continue to walk in every day. God's love continues to perfect and establish my worth strongly in Him. My identity is not crafted or determined by people or circumstances. It's not determined by how people choose to relate with me or not relate at all.

Though at times, it may seem as if I am alone when people deny or withhold the simplest form of relationship; reciprocation -the air and fuel that centers our relationships. My self-worth is deeply rooted in the way God sees me and says about me. The steering wheel for my destiny and purpose. He continues to have the final word in my life regarding everything.

The Bible teaches that God is omnipresent. God is everywhere we go and everywhere we cannot. David acknowledges, *"Where can I go from your Spirit? Where can I flee from your presence? If I go up to the heavens, you are there; if I make my bed in the depths, you are there. If I rise on the wings of the dawn, if I settle on the far side of the sea, even there your hand will guide me, your right hand will hold me fast,"* (Psalm 139:7–10 ESV)

God's presence is ever-present in my life. He is always with me, whether my mind and body or people around me acknowledge it. I am secure in his love; his peace is unspeakable amid life's storms. So, as you read this short chapter, let him be your rest as you discover your worth in the eyes of the King.

He desires to make you whole, he gave his only son for your mind, body, and spirit to be at rest. Find time to be grateful for all He has done for you. Allow yourself to get lost in acknowledging his presence, which leaves no time to think about why others seem so far or none existent.

As you go through life, let the presence of God be a reminder of what a friend you have in him! Begin to acknowledge God in everything you do, everywhere you go. In no time you will realize the need for others to communicate or reach out will slowly and eventually dissipate. Settle yourself in solitude and find God's presence.

You are made for so much more. It's more than the job you do, the business you run, the family you manage, the connections you share with others. It's more and deep, it's about acknowledging the creator and sovereign God. Your relationship with him will settle you amid the daily hustle and bustle of life.

Your life will have meaning and the peace that flows with connecting with your maker is unspeakable. Your relationship with the king of kings opens the doors that have been closed. It clears the fog of uncertainty that could be clouding your day. It sets you up for victory every single day no matter what is thrown at you. You are confident in his guiding hand and his ever presence. Settle in His Presence, there is peace and love there.

Word Nugget

The bible is the word of God. It is life and has the power to bring change and healing in your life. The word of God is designed to nourish the soul and spirit in the same way food nourishes the body. Spend some time reading this scripture, read out loud and memorize, if possible. As you meditate on the scripture, take inventory and any observations regarding your personal life.

Isaiah 26:3 says, *"You will keep in perfect peace those whose minds are steadfast because they trust in you."*

Food for Thought

Is your mind stayed on him, what are you spending time thinking about? How are you spending your alone time? Are you focused on the issues around you or looking for an opportunity to stay unstuck and tapped into the vein of life, Jesus Christ?

9

God's Wisdom
Wait on the Wind Thermals

As you walk in God's divine wisdom, you will surely begin to see a greater measure of victory and good success in your life.
-Joseph Prince

Would it make a difference if you understood that your life is and has always been God's plan A, designed specifically for you? What if knowing that your life is part of His wise plan would that affect your confidence in God and how you live your life?

To know the will of God is the highest of Wisdom. Wisdom, especially spiritual wisdom, is not just about knowing what's good for you, but applying that knowledge into your everyday life. When you do that, you begin to understand the plan of God for your life. Wisdom is the most important quality for success in life. With success, we achieve goals, experience the fullness of life and find a purpose for our lives.

Wisdom is the ability to discern and make good judgments based on what you have learned from experiences or the knowledge and understanding that gives you this ability. It's knowing the meaning or the reason; why something is, and what it means to your life.

Wisdom sees the big picture in focus, each part in its proper relational place of rest. Wisdom *"is more profitable than silver and yields better returns than gold"* (Proverbs 3:14). Wisdom *"is more pre-*

cious than rubies" (Proverbs 3:15). Wisdom fortifies every aspect of your life and sets everything in your life on a firm foundation.

Wisdom is an attribute of God. Listen to the psalmist, *"His understanding is infinite,"* (Psalm 147:5). Jeremiah prays to the *"great and mighty God whose name is the Lord of Hosts, the One great in counsel and mighty in deed, whose eyes are on all the ways of the sons of men to give to each person according to his ways and the result of his deeds."* (Jeremiah 32:19).

Daniel describes God's wisdom, *"He changes the times and seasons; He removes kings and establishes kings. He gives wisdom to the wise and knowledge to those who have an understanding. He reveals the deep and hidden things; He knows what is in the darkness, and light dwells with Him."* (Dan. 2:21-22) Nothing's ever a mystery to God. He is never puzzled or confused or uncertain.

Paul writes about the wisdom of God, and when he does, it moves to praise: *"Oh, the depth of the riches of the wisdom and knowledge of God! How unsearchable his judgments, and his paths beyond tracing out! Who has known the mind of the Lord? Or who has been his counselor? Who has ever given to God, that God should repay them? For from him and through him and for him are all things. To him be the glory forever! Amen."* (Rom. 11:33-36)

Did you get that last part? For from Him and through Him and to Him are all things. To Him be the glory forever. Paul wants us to be certain about one thing, God's wisdom is illimitable—so vast that His judgments are unsearchable. God's wisdom is colossal that His ways are untraceable. We can't follow what He's doing without being hopelessly over our head. It is so boundless that no one has been or could be His counselor, ever.

The wisdom of God is immeasurable and expansive that He does not and cannot increase in wisdom. To have this kind of wisdom is to have the heartbeat of God. It is having the awareness of God.

Is the wisdom of God-given to mankind? Many verses reveal that God does indeed gift us with His wisdom. None is perhaps well known for wisdom like King Solomon. I Kings 4:29 says God gave Solomon wisdom and great insight, and a breadth of understanding as measureless as the sand on the seashore.

When you understand that the wisdom of God is the mind of God. And as a Christian, you have the mind of God. Then it's liberating to know that while people and situations may consistently change around you, or may bring uncertainty every day, the things that truly matter will never change. God's promises are true, and his word is a sure foundation.

The bible says, wisdom will *"keep you; love her, and she will guard you"* (Proverbs 4:6 ESV). Wisdom will *"prolong your life"*, *"bring you prosperity"* (Proverbs 3:2). *"win you the favor and a good name in the sight of God and man"* (Proverbs 3:4), and *"make your paths straight"* (Proverbs 3:6). Wisdom is essential in how we handle deals, make investments or run households and businesses.

Wisdom is fundamental to us living victoriously. It gives us the ability to discern the best way to navigate through situations and issues in our lives. Wisdom provides us with the ability to integrate, to coalesce different factors from various sources of knowledge and experiences in life.

Without wisdom, life can be vexatious. Our human wisdom can lead us into more trouble, life can seem very unfair. If life contained perfect justice, every one of us would suffer eternally for every shortcoming in our imperfect lives. It is better than fair that a righteous Savior would bridge the gap between imperfect man and a perfect God with infinite wisdom.

Most turmoil in life flows from foolishness, and foolishness from a lack of wisdom. To avoid being foolish and thus being defeated in life, seek wisdom. Pursue wisdom with all you've got. Like all other gifts from God, the gift awaits those who value it and desire to seek after it. It will not fall from up above, we must desire wisdom. Wisdom is acquired, not inherited. It is attained, not discovered.

James writes on the qualities of wisdom, *"But the wisdom that comes from heaven is pure, then peace-loving, considerate, sub-*

missive, full of mercy and good fruit, impartial and sincere," (James 3:17). Take full stock of these qualities of wisdom, they will help you understand the worth of wisdom.

This wisdom described by James is having the heartbeat of God. This kind of understanding is to have an awareness of God. However, you cannot just acquire this wisdom, you must seek and pursue it. To seek the wisdom of God is the answer to every individual. If we turn our hearts to Him and allow His Word to guide us, we will live a life embraced with God's love and wisdom.

No matter what we encounter in life, we will be equipped to handle life's curveballs. God's wisdom elevates and guides us. When Gods' mind is imparted to us through wisdom, there is greater success in everything we do. Wisdom is available to those who value it and intentionally pursue it.

"To know wisdom and instruction, to understand words of insight, to receive instruction in wise dealing, in righteousness, justice, and equity. To give prudence to the simple, knowledge and discretion to the youth. Let the wise hear and increase in learning, and the one who understands obtain guidance, to understand a proverb and a saying, the words of the wise and their riddles. The fear of the Lord is the beginning of knowledge; fools despise wisdom and instruction," (Proverbs 1:2-7).

Blessed is the one who finds wisdom, the one who attains understanding, for she is more profitable than silver and yields better returns than gold. She is more precious than rubies; nothing you desire can compare to her. Long-life is in her right hand; in her left hand are riches and honor. Her ways are pleasant, and all her paths are peace. She is a tree of life to those who embrace her; those who lay hold of her will be blessed.

Commit yourself to the pursuit of God's wisdom and cherish it above life's distractions. If attained, wisdom can become the most prized possession of your life. More than any other virtue, wisdom can bring success, happiness, peace, and confidence. Wisdom should be at the forefront of your core values. It is that important

Determine to seek wisdom from God and embrace it. I've learned that I can never rise above the level of wisdom I have achieved. Foolishness is obvious, but wisdom is discreet. Wisdom is acquired, not inherited. It is attained, not discovered. Wisdom is important, it's tied to your success, as you journey to get unstuck and thrive in life.

James reminds us *"If any of you lacks wisdom, you should ask God, who gives generously to all without finding fault, and it will be given to you,"* (James 1:5).

PART 4

Soar Again

10

Celebrate You–
You are Designed to be Limitless

You don't become what you want, you become what you believe.
-Oprah Winfrey

Every day, we are engulfed with the demands of life, the daily hustle and bustle, media-crazed images, and opinions of others. These demands dictate while stripping off our identity, dreams of creating, exploring and living deeply. We are merely existing and going through the motions of life. We consistently allow fear to overwhelm us while watching life pass by.

The truth is, along the voyage of life perhaps during childhood or young adulthood or in marriage we've learned to mask our God-given traits to the extent we now live a lie. Instead of fulfillment in life, feelings of frustration, restlessness and even anxiety have inundated our day-to-day life. We seem to like the idea of being true to ourselves, but almost like a reflex, we simply "want to fit in" and conform to what everyone else is doing, forgetting our value.

Do you know who you are? Do you portray who you are on the inside? Do you take time to celebrate who you are? Does the world get to see the real you? Does it even matter if you are authentic?

You know that you have been called to do more but don't know exactly what it is? Are you trying to figure out life? How do you define yourself? If you've been asking these questions over time, it's time to unpack the real you. It's time to release the guilt, the need to fit in and be what others want you to be.

Refuse to become like everyone else, a copycat. Do not settle into what others say, allowing their comments to strip you of the unique characteristics that make you authentic and remarkable. Refuse to open the door to a lifestyle of confusion, distortion, mediocrity, and complacency.

To live authentically, you must first learn how to be yourself; this means living with a deep sense of who you are and what you have been created to be. Knowing and embracing your value, celebrating whom God created you to be.

> *"When nobody else celebrates you, learn to celebrate yourself. When nobody else compliments you, then compliment yourself. It's not up to other people to keep you encouraged. It's up to you. Encouragement should come from the inside," -Joel Osteen*

Your journey is to rediscover your magnificence on many levels. You are to become the fullest expression of whom you were created to be, full of purpose and passion not the opinions of others. To walk this out, you are to know your value. It's impossible to know your value unless you truly believe you are valuable.

You must realize that the thoughts and images you focus on re-enforce who you are. What you focus on, you become. When your thoughts are filled with dreams of creativity, images of exploration and living deeply, you cultivate feelings of worth and value.

Over time, I've discovered these practical suggestions that have radically inspired me to live purposefully and authentically (ability to be real!)

Guard your mind: We are daily barraged with information, images, and opinions of others which can be overwhelming. Whether we are aware of it or not, this information affects our thoughts and perspectives. We need to become intentional about not conforming or accepting everything that comes at you. We must clear the outside clatter that interferes with the uniqueness on the inside of us.

Embrace your potential: Anytime I'm faced with new challenges or situations. I strive to review each challenge through the lens of God's word and my ability in Christ, not my current limitations. Philippians 4:13 reminds me, *"I can do all things through Christ who strengthens me."*

My experience has been when I trust in the Lord and embrace my ability to grow and become better. It's easier to shrug off public opinion and self-doubt, which allows me to become the best version of myself. Solomon said, *"Trust in the Lord with all your heart and lean not unto your own understanding. In all your ways acknowledge him, and he shall direct your paths"* (Proverbs 3:5,6)

Make authentic decisions: I have learned that my actions become my habits, and my habits become my character. When my character is consistent with my values, making authentic decisions becomes second nature to me. The core values that guide my actions and decisions every day are rooted in the word of God.

Trouble comes when we make decisions based on the opinions of others, our circumstances, or what others do. Psalm 1:1 Blessed is the one who does not walk in step with the wicked or stand in the way that sinners take or sit in the company of mockers. Be careful about the people you allow into your life. Everything they carry around could cause you to make right or wrong decisions.

Infuse your day with gratitude: In Colossians 2:7, Paul says that we are to be *"overflowing with gratitude."* Several years ago, I made the decision to begin or end each day with several things that I'm grateful for. I've found that the more I appreciate what I have, who I am, the more fulfilling my life becomes.

You must garnish the courage to be strong in Christ, where you abide in him including your imperfections! You must believe that you are worthy of love, just as you are. Be willing to be adventurous, listen to your inner wisdom, experience your inner power, permit yourself to be you, be vulnerable and believe that you deserve to be celebrated.

I refuse to walk outside my blessing to fit in or to make others comfortable. I am comfortable in who God created me to be. A woman in a class all by myself. A limited-edition. A woman who always wins despite life's obstacles and knows that her identity is rooted in Christ.

Let me encourage you to walk in the blessing of who you are. Be yourself. Let them get over it, whoever they are. You are magnificent! You are the beloved of God. A victor and conqueror in every aspect of your life. You have been created to win in all levels of life.

Thank you for making me so wonderfully complex! It is amazing to think about. Your workmanship is marvelous—and how well I know it. — Psalm 139:14 (TLB)

11
Grace Wins–
The Beauty of Form Under the Influence of Freedom

Grace is the beauty of form under the influence of freedom.
-Friedrich Schiller

We all have moments where we are not proud of how we've handled a situation or how we acted. However, when you are grounded in who you are, you have a certain essence where people sense that not much moves you. Many of us are emotionally out of control, lacking the presence of mind, allowing life to take us on an emotional roller coaster where we feel crazy and at the mercy of our life situations, people and emotions.

In her book, *The Resolution for Women,* Priscilla Shirer writes "Grace, by definition, is favor or kindness expressed to the undeserving. It means giving someone a break when it's the last thing they deserve to get, and it is precisely what was given to us by God Himself when He extended to us salvation from our sins, even though we were dreadfully sinful."

When you receive God's grace—His gift to you, the realization of just how much he forgives and forgets your mistakes every single day, you find the motivation to extend the same undeserved favor to those around you. Ephesians 2:8 reminds us, for it is by grace you have been saved, through faith—and this is not from yourselves, it is the gift of God.

And when people in your life know that you won't look down on them or hold their inadequacies over them, you have given them a great gift. It's an overflow of the gift given to you by God. The gift of being able to stay authentic, knowing they'll be accepted just as they are.

Isn't that how you want to feel yourself? And isn't that the kind of freedom you want others to experience in their relationship with you?

Grace givers are those who chose to perceive the best, even when the worst is illuminated. They resolve to let the people in their homes and life enjoy what they have instead of focusing on what they don't. They are those who don't want people walking on pins and needles around them, always having to accommodate their emotional mood swings or cover up their failures for fear of being misunderstood?

Priscilla Shirer bluntly expresses that "Grace overwhelms. Everywhere it appears. Just think what it might accomplish when it comes gushing through your smile, your hug, your kiss, your tender pat on the back, your wink of forgiveness." Grace releases, frees, relaxes, loosens nerves, gives permission and room to express acceptance.

Grace is the oil that lubricates friction and relieves tension. Grace is the smile that everyone you love is waiting to receive from you—so that they can finally be themselves around you. Like you were, when Jesus graced your life.

To be graceful means that you know who you are and are grounded and comfortable in that person. The person that has been shown mercy and kindness, time and time again. The person that willingly gives grace over and over and chooses to look at everything through the lens of grace.

Word Nugget

The word of God is designed to nourish the soul and spirit in the same way food nourishes the body. Spend some time reading the scriptures. As you meditate on the scripture, take inventory and any observations regarding your personal life.

2 Corinthians 8:7 *But as you excel in everything—in faith, in speech, in knowledge, in all earnestness, and in our love for you—see that you excel in this act of grace also*

Proverbs 15:1 *A gentle answer turns away anger, but a harsh word stirs up wrath.*

Romans 12:3 *For by the grace given me I say to every one of you: Do not think of yourself more highly than you ought, but think of yourself with sober judgment, according to the measure of faith God has given you*

Food for Thought

For a moment, step out of the day-to-day struggles and your feelings, and look at the grand scheme of things. Are you easy to be around? Do you make it natural for your loved ones to sense acceptance? Do you keep track of their mistakes and failures? Do you hold others captive to your critical nature?

Spend some time reviewing these thought-provoking questions. And while you meditate upon them, be honest with yourself and make notes about anything you may observe about your personal life and any changes you may want to make. Do those around get to see a smile of gratitude brighten your face when they do something to please you, or do you hardly even notice? Do people around you walk on eggshells?

If your attention is primarily wrapped in thoughts that are unhealthy, selfish and ungodly around your loved ones and close relations. Give them a break. I know they don't deserve it. But neither did you. Grace came anyway into your life.

12

Break Free
Flight of Rebirth

You will never change your life until you change something you do daily.
-Mike Murdock

Relationships are a necessary part of healthy living, but there is no such thing as a perfect relationship. Relationships have the potential to enrich our lives and add to our enjoyment of life. However, these same relationships can cause us discomfort, and sometimes even cause harm.

A healthy relationship should bring more happiness than turmoil into your life. Every relationship will have stress at times, but you want to prevent prolonged mental stress on either member of the relationship.

Healthy relationships should foster a safe place where both partners can work toward genuine friendship, where communication, boundaries, respect, truth, and trust flow back and forth. They allow parties involved to feel supported and connected but still feel independent.

Unhealthy relationships can leave us feeling uncomfortable, sad, and afraid. It is very difficult for people to let the realization set in that perhaps a friend, co-worker or family member isn't treating them well or respectful, as they should be. It can be even more difficult when the person treating them this way is a loved one.

This doesn't mean if someone treats you badly or you have a disagreement that the relationship is automatically unhealthy. Disagreements happen in healthy relationships all the time. Most often what makes a relationship healthy is the need and the act of compromising when disagreements occur.

Relationships that are not healthy are marred by power and control, not equality and respect. When arguments happen, a person is always made to feel bad about themselves; where ridicule and name-calling are the norm. Where possessiveness, insults, jealous accusations, yelling, humiliation, pulling and tagging or other abusive behaviors, are at their root exertions of power and control.

It saddens me to see single adults, especially those who have been waiting a while to find a marriage partner, end up in unhealthy relationships, which so often lead to spiritual and moral compromise, bad marriages and divorces.

It ultimately takes your decision to start the process of breaking free from unhealthy relationships. The decision to break free can be painful and difficult, but it is infinitely less painful in the long run than staying. You must decide if you are committed to your comfort zone or if you want to be committed to your happiness, joy, and freedom.

Are you currently stuck in unhealthy relationships? Are all your relationships healthy? Do you find yourself stuck with thoughts from previous relationships; unable to move forward or break free from the vicious cycle of unhealthy relationships?

The truth of the matter is your soul is tied to these relationships. We all need to be very careful who and what our soul ties to. Why? Because living with an ungodly or unhealthy relational soul tie will pour cold water on our life's purpose and plan. We can become powerless, sadly addicted and living in bondage if we do not manage soul ties.

Your soul is made up of your mind, your will, and your emotions; it is your inner life. A soul tie is an emotional connection or a bond with another that unites you. Soul ties are not necessarily bad. After all, God created them. They can be good if it's something that God wants for your life. Any relationship (s) you form can either build you up or tear you down.

Whenever you spend time with anyone, you develop an emotional connection that unites you and creates soul tie. The more intimate (close, private and personal, closely acquainted; familiar) you are, the stronger the soul ties. Soul ties are responsible for the pain you sense when a relationship ends. They have deceived young people looking for love, married adults flirting with disaster, and abused women and men trapped in a vicious cycle.

To sever negative soul ties is a difficult and daunting task. It is what you think, what you want and what you feel. You may have ended a physically intimate relationship months ago, but you still sense a pull toward that person. Why? Because there is a soul tie. Soul ties prevent us from moving on to new relationships, even the ones God may be leading us into.

It's time for you to break negative or wrong soul ties to pursue your purpose. There are several things you can do to help you break free from these soul ties that God wants you to get free of.

Make a quality decision to please God more than anyone. You have one life to live, and it matters to God. You cannot live your life displeasing God to please someone else. This will lead you to a life of deep regret. Realize, you need to come to the place in your life where pleasing God is the most important thing to you. To give anyone that much influence as God should have in your life opens the door for Satan to come into your life. He will make it so much harder for you to give up this soul tie. The right time to break free, detach and cut the strings is now.

Determine to spend time in the Word of God. Meditation on God's word will empower you to develop the strength to sever an ungodly soul tie. You cannot do this on your own. You will want to fill yourself with God's word which helps you in making better decisions. It must be a part of your strategic plan to be free of your past. The Bible is your greatest weapon against Satan. He does not want you to break your soul ties. He is desperately working to keep you locked into this situation. The devil will lie to you and convince you that you cannot live without the person. Just like anything else, you won't see results overnight. You must make studying the Word a habit.

Free yourself from that relationship: You need to free yourself from that relationship or person to whom you have ungodly soul ties. Detach yourself of this wrong soul tie until you no longer miss him or her. And listen to this: there will come a day when you will no longer miss that person. This is the hardest part, but you can do it.

Challenge

Review your current and past relationships to determine where could you be tangled up with unhealthy soul ties that need to be untangled. With the help of some nuggets outlined above coupled with the word of God. Focus on freeing yourself from the web of toxic, unhealthy soul ties.

God designed each of us with unique gifts, talents, and interests. When we discover and nurture those gifts, we experience a great sense of joy and satisfaction. We then bring that joy and energy into our relationships. Everyone benefits because we aren't relying on one another or our ever-changing roles to define our entire existence. We are free to explore the whole-hearted life God wants for us.

Life will bring a steady stream of changes. So as the seasons' change, we have to be intentional about discovering and pursuing our passions. It's an ongoing process that keeps us growing and our relationships healthy and vibrant.

Let me point you to Terri Savelle Foy book "Untangle". In this book, she unveils more information on breaking wrong soul ties and how to focus on pursuing your purpose.

13

Birth New Dreams
Rise To Greater Heights

All our dreams can come true, if we have the courage to pursue them.
-Walt Disney

We've all been at this place in life, where it all seems so distorted and foggy. Nothing seems pleasing to the eye, the nights seemed longer and days shorter. It appears like you can't seem to catch a break or move on to the next season.

Does life at times seem to be stagnant, full of uncertainties and lack clarity? Are you wondering why your dreams are not fulfilling? Do you feel like you can hardly catch a break in life? Why are God's promises not being fulfilled in your life?

The good news is the word of God is full of promises about your life. If you are determined to spend quality time in the word of God; the time spent in the word yields results. Changes will begin to happen all around you; new ideas, perspectives, clarity in your vision and purpose in life.

"The secret of your future is hidden in your daily routine,"-Mike Murdock

At the time I encountered this quote, coupled with the knowledge of God's word, I determined that my life would never be the same again. You see, his plans and purpose for your life are to prosper and not harm you, but to give you hope and a future. He predetermined this plan for your life before the foundation of the world. He is constantly birthing new dreams within you, but you need to partake in his plan.

> *"Behold, I am doing a new thing; now it springs forth, do you not perceive it? I will make a way in the wilderness and rivers in the desert."* -Isaiah 43:19

Open your heart and tune in as you perceive the new things God is birthing inside of you. It takes incorporating simple yet purposeful changes into your daily routine. These newly created routines will propel you to establish new habits. Every new habit you learn and establish is a conduit for birthing new things, ideas, disciplines, behaviors, and attitudes.

We can adapt to simple new disciplines and routines, coupled with the word of God. You can begin with a simple change in your morning routine like establishing a daily connection with the source of your life and strength—God. Romans 8:28 reminds us that *"God causes all things to work together for good to those who love God, to those who are called according to His purpose."*

Several years back, I determined to create new routines in my life. Each morning, I woke up early for a 30-minute walk. I added listening to a motivational word while preparing for work. As much as I enjoyed reading books, I moved to the next level, reading a chapter a day. These new routines propelled me to a new focus, perspectives and ideas.

You can do the same, take ten to twenty minutes each day walking outside—this could alter how your body functions, your metabolism could change. You could add reading a book or learning a new language, taking cooking classes. So, what is holding you back from fulfilling your destiny and creating new experiences?

Isaiah prophesied, In the same way, I will not cause pain without allowing something new to be born," says the Lord. *"If I cause you the pain, I will not stop you from giving birth to your new nation,"* says your God. Isaiah 66:9 (NCV). Is there pain in your life currently? Are you going through some of your worst experiences in life?

If so, God's word is true and a sure foundation. No matter life's painful moments. There is potential, an opportunity for something new to be incorporated into your life that will change your circumstances. Allow yourself to acknowledge the pain, but not dwell on it, purpose to make some changes in your life. Review lessons learned from your current situation or difficult season.

Begin forming new habits, while making lasting changes by trying something new. Determine today to start a new routine, a new approach; It may be setting time aside weekly or biweekly to soak in a warm bathtub while listening to music. It could be a short or long stroll outside after work. Give yourself permission to feel the air brush through your hair and blow on your cheeks while you admire God's beautiful creation.

What are you willing to do to get unstuck and look at things from a different perspective? Forget the former things, the painful memories and look forward to the new season. Review the reasons for stagnation in your life; unwillingness to form new habits, why you are stuck in your old ways, and unfulfilling routines.

Word Nugget

Use the word of God to purposely remain focused on getting unstuck. Reject the notion of settling into painful seasons. The determination to invest in yourself before you can invest in others allows you to change situations that may present in your life. The power remains within you to bring about change and newness.

Isaiah 42:9 ESV *Behold, the former things have come to pass, and new things I now declare; before they spring forth I tell you of them.*

Isaiah 65:17 AMP *For behold, I create new heavens and a new earth. And the former things shall not be remembered or come into mind.*

Food for Thought

Introspection: What current routine has you stuck at this moment? What bad habits are you cycling day after day?

Unless you change, nothing will change in your current life situation. If you want to become more, you must do more. Something new can be birthed inside of you each day if you choose to make changes. Resolve today to establish new habits and change something in your daily routine. Five simple things that you can do daily to invest in yourself before you invest in others.

Your life is too precious and too valuable to God for you to waste it on the wrong purpose. The time is now to get serious. Challenge yourself to remain consistent. Consistency is the key to change in every area of your life. Set a target date to maintain the new simple habits you form. Remain focused and determined to get unstuck. To get unstuck and live a victorious life, you must hold yourself accountable.

Step out of your comfort zone and mediocre lifestyle to become victorious in life. Changing routines one day at a time.

"The future belongs to those who believe in the beauty of their dreams."
-Eleanor Roosevelt

Dream Again!

It's time to get unstuck, embrace your purpose and thrive in life.

Dreams bring life, healing, and a new perspective. It's time to dream again, when is the last time you dreamed about your future? It's time to begin a new routine that will propel you to think differently, have a fresh perspective about life. It's time to start walking in your God-ordained purpose and birth the new dreams. It's time to flourish and become the best version of yourself. It's time to forget the former things and press forward towards the mark of the high calling. This is just the beginning of what God wants to do in your life.

Forever Victorious!

Notes:

Notes:

Notes:

Notes:

Notes:

Notes:

Notes:

Notes:

About the Author

Lillian is passionate about living a life of purpose and authenticity (the ability to be real!). A writer, motivator, change-agent, and influential leader fueled by her passion to embrace, empower and educate women through thought-provoking questions, practical suggestions, sharing of her struggles and a solid foundation in the Word of God. Her strongest influence is the ability to temper God's wisdom coupled with humility to share encouraging victorious word-packed insights with women from all aspects of life.

Like an eagle, she embraces opportunities, life experiences and the unwavering acceptance of transformation by the word of God. She envelopes the multiple, broken places and pieces of her life with grace and humility. Grateful that time and time again, the grace of God has made her whole. Over time, she has learned to welcome all seasons of life and the experiences afforded to her; acknowledging that she is forever victorious!

She is a compassionate warrior who will encourage you to fight for your dreams no matter what obstacles you are facing. She desires to inspire you to live intentionally; adapting a focused mindset that your destiny is not tied to those who left or opportunities and people who have closed doors on you. Lillian believes that all women have a story that waits to be told and a secret that would rather not be told. She is driven to motivate women to seize opportunities to share their stories and embrace the freedom that unlocks doors of bondage, fear, and guilt. She empowers women like you with life-changing applicable knowledge of God's word.

She has been involved in Christian Ministry all her life. She began earlier in age beside her parents who Pastor in Nairobi, Kenya. She continues to support her local church, CityLife Church in Tampa, Florida. She has learned the guiding principles of the word of God and as a Beyond Discipleship facilitator, she enjoys sharing with other Christian adults the importance of following God's blueprint for spiritual development. She cherishes the opportunity to connect with fellow women as a Connect group leader focusing on creating a space, where women can share and embrace their God-given purpose as they journey their Christian life together.

Lillian is a community advocate that supports various community service initiatives and has served on overseas mission trips. She serves as Vice-Chair for the board of directors at Premier Community Healthcare Center in Hernando and Pasco Counties. In addition to her family, community, and church, she leads highly influential teams responsible for providing strategic guidance and delivering value on cutting edge solutions with integration of systems at the intersection of healthcare and IT. A thought healthcare IT leader with a background in engineering and years of experience in the healthcare IT industry solving complex systems and workflows integration that benefits patients and providers.

Lastly, Lillian is the founder of Brilliance. A women's empowerment group with a mission to inspire, impart and influence women to step out of the shadows and to invest in themselves, network and share with others while uplifting and supporting one another. She continues to be a strong supporter of women thriving at home, at work while empowering them to be community leaders as much as they've been family matriarchs.

www.ingramcontent.com/pod-product-compliance
Lightning Source LLC
Chambersburg PA
CBHW022010120526
44592CB00034B/765